The Gift

Graham Kendrick

MAKE WAY MUSIC

kevin mayhew

We hope you enjoy *The Gift*. Further copies are available from your local Kevin Mayhew stockist.

In case of difficulty, or to request a catalogue, please contact the publisher direct by writing to:

The Sales Department
KEVIN MAYHEW LTD
Buxhall
Stowmarket
Suffolk IP14 3BW

Phone 01449 737978
Fax 01449 737834
E-mail info@kevinmayhewltd.com

© Copyright Make Way Music 1988
PO Box 263, Croydon, Surrey CR9 5AP, UK
www.makewaymusic.com

First published 1988
Reprinted 1989
Reprinted 1992
Reprinted 1994
Reprinted 1995
Reprinted 1998
Reprinted 2002

Marketed and distributed by Kevin Mayhew Ltd.

ISBN 1 84003 963 9
ISMN M 57024 118 7
Catalogue No: 1450259

0 1 2 3 4 5 6 7 8 9

Original illustration by Peter Rogers
Cover design by Angela Selfe

Music setter: Geoffrey Moore
Music proof reader: Marian Hellen

Printed and bound in Great Britain

Important Copyright Information

The Publishers wish to express their gratitude to the copyright owners who have granted permission to include their copyright material in this book. Full details are indicated on the respective pages.

The **words** of most of the songs in this publication are covered by a **Church Copyright Licence** which is available from Christian Copyright Licensing International. This allows local church reproduction on overhead projector acetates, in service bulletins, songsheets, audio/visual recording and other formats.

The **music** in this book is covered by the additional **Music Reproduction Licence** which is issued by CCLI in the territories of Europe and Australasia. You may photocopy the music and words of the songs in the book provided:

You hold a current Music Reproduction Licence from CCLI.

The copyright owner of the song you intend to photocopy is included in the Authorised Catalogue List which comes with your Music Reproduction Licence.

The Music Reproduction Licence is **not** currently available in the USA or Canada.

Full details of CCLI can be obtained from their Web site (www.ccli.com) or you can contact them direct at the following offices:

Christian Copyright Licensing (Europe) Ltd
PO Box 1339, Eastbourne, East Sussex, BN21 1AD, UK
Tel: +44 (0)1323 417711; Fax: +44 (0)1323 417722; E-mail: info@ccli.co.uk

CCL Asia-Pacific Pty Ltd (Australia and New Zealand)
PO Box 6644, Baulkham Hills Business Centre, NSW 2153, Australia
Tel: +61 (02) 9894-5386; Toll Free Phone: 1-800-635-474
Fax: +61 (02) 9894-5701; Toll Free Fax: 1-800-244-477
E-mail executive@ccli.co.au

Christian Copyright Licensing Inc
17201 NE Sacramento Street, Portland, Oregon 97230, USA
Tel: +1 (503) 257 2230; Toll Free Phone: 1 (800) 234 2446;
Fax: +1 (503) 257 2244; E-mail executive@ccli.com

Please note, all texts and music in this book are protected by copyright and if you do not possess a licence from CCLI they may not be reproduced in any way for sale or private use without the consent of the copyright owner.

Contents

Part 1: Celebrating the Gift

	Page
Introduction (Tonight)	8
Tonight (Glory to God)	9
The Christmas Child	14
The Servant King (From heaven you came)	16
Let it be to me	18
Immanuel, O Immanuel	19
Thanks be to God	23
O what a mystery I see	26
Tell out, tell out the news	30
The Candle Song	32

Part 2: Sharing the Gift

Introduction (Good News)	34
Good News	34
Sing all the earth	37
Gloria	39
Arise, shine	40
This Child	44
O come and join the dance	46
Introduction (The Giving Song)	48
The Giving Song	49
For God so loved the world	50
Peace to you	52
God with us	53
Heaven invites you to a party	56
Tonight (Glory to God) – reprise	61
Thanks be to God – reprise	64

Words

Part 1: Celebrating the Gift	68
Part 2: Sharing the Gift	72

I hate Christmas!

There have been moments of frustration when I have been tempted to utter such words, and I am sure that I am not alone in this. I remember some years ago returning from a visit to India, and arriving two or three days before Christmas Day, and rushing out to buy some last-minute presents. The contrast between the pitiful slums of Bombay and the bustling gift shops of the South of England was hard to cope with in the same twenty-four hours, and I found no way to reconcile the two extremes.

Yet love it or hate it, Christmas is here to stay, and if we can extricate ourselves from its more debilitating effects it offers enormous opportunities to announce the real good news, which is not how much people are spending in the shops, but how much God spent on us when he sent his Son in the likeness of sinful flesh.

The Gift has a few important differences from the previous Make Way marches, *A Carnival of Praise* and *Shine, Jesus, Shine*. Part two can be used on a street procession in the normal way, but it is also designed as a static event, indoors or outdoors. It is intended as the basis for a joyful Christmas celebration, a kind of 'Christmas party for Jesus', and it is up to your own ingenuity to adapt it for shopping precincts, halls, schools, neighbourhood streets, carol services and so on. When used indoors, part one is very suitable as the opening of a whole evening event.

As well as being a vehicle for proclamation, praise and worship, it aims to help us build a bridge to unbelievers for whom the Christmas story may be little more than a myth and sentiment, a fairy tale with no relevance to the real world. However, behind the glitter and television glamour, the real world of Christmas is often an unhappy and stressful time for many people. It can become a focus for financial pressures, family tensions and loneliness, and the traditional over-indulgence and cynical materialism can leave people feeling very empty.

For others of course it is a happy time, but being temporarily happy is no substitute for being eternally secure in Christ's forgiveness. After all, the purpose of the incarnation was to save people from their sins, not just to make them happy.

Into this spiritual and often physical poverty, *The Gift* is designed to help us announce the 'greatest gift of all' in an atmosphere of joyful praise. Many generations before Christ's birth, it was announced by the prophet that he would be called 'Immanuel' which means 'God with us'. My hope is that these songs will provide a framework for an experience of 'God with us' as we invite people to join the 'party' that will go on into eternity.

Graham Kendrick

Part 1
CELEBRATING THE GIFT

Introduction (Tonight)

Graham Kendrick

© Copyright 1988 Make Way Music, P.O. Box 263, Croydon, Surrey CR9 5AP, UK.
International copyright secured. All rights reserved. Used by permission.

Tonight
Glory to God

Words and Music: Graham Kendrick

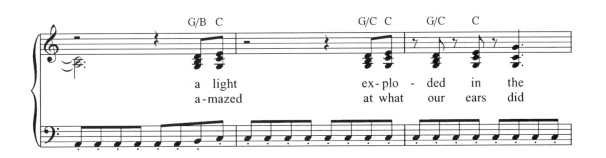

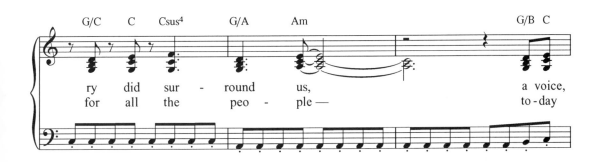

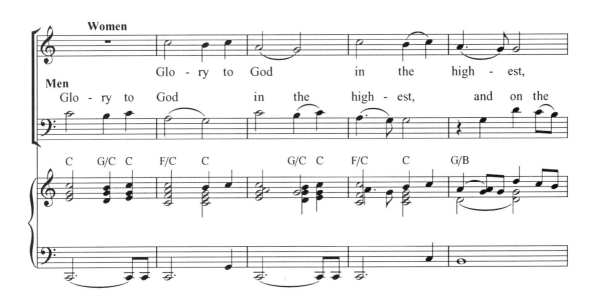

The Christmas Child

Words and Music: Graham Kendrick

© Copyright 1988 Make Way Music, P.O. Box 263, Croydon, Surrey CR9 5AP, UK.
International copyright secured. All rights reserved. Used by permission.

The Servant King
From heaven you came

Words and Music: Graham Kendrick

Slowly, with feeling

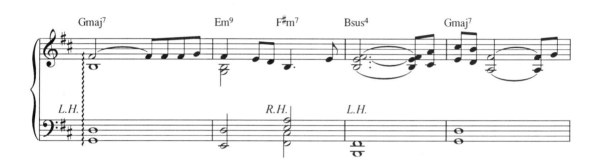
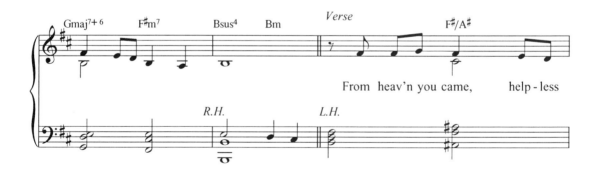

© Copyright 1983 Thankyou Music/Adm. by worshiptogether.com songs excl. UK & Europe, adm. by Kingsway Music. tym@kingsway.co.uk. Used by permission.

Let it be to me

Words and Music: Graham Kendrick

Immanuel, O Immanuel

Words and Music: Graham Kendrick

Worshipfully, but with strength

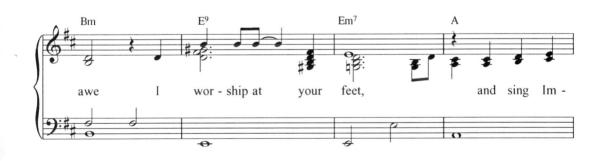

© Copyright 1988 Make Way Music, P.O. Box 263, Croydon, Surrey CR9 5AP, UK.
International copyright secured. All rights reserved. Used by permission.

Thanks be to God

Words and Music: Graham Kendrick

© Copyright 1988 Make Way Music, P.O. Box 263, Croydon, Surrey CR9 5AP, UK.
International copyright secured. All rights reserved. Used by permission.

O what a mystery I see

Words and Music: Graham Kendrick

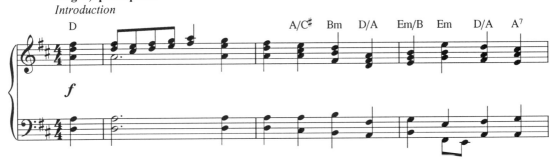

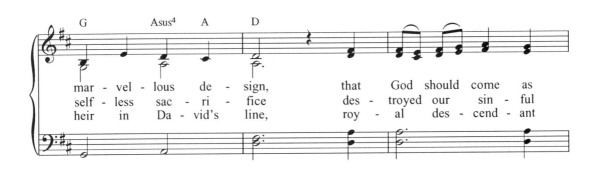

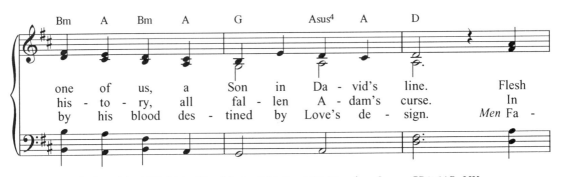

© Copyright 1988 Make Way Music, P.O. Box 263, Croydon, Surrey CR9 5AP, UK.
International copyright secured. All rights reserved. Used by permission.

Tell out, tell out the news

Words and Music: Graham Kendrick

© Copyright 1988 Make Way Music, P.O. Box 263, Croydon, Surrey CR9 5AP, UK.
International copyright secured. All rights reserved. Used by permission.

The Candle Song

Words and Music: Graham Kendrick

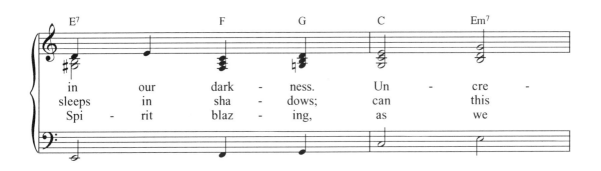

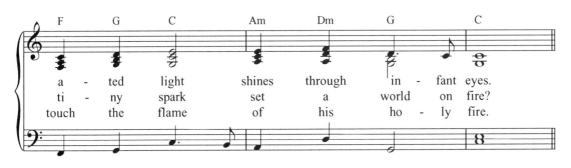

© Copyright 1988 Make Way Music, P.O. Box 263, Croydon, Surrey CR9 5AP, UK.
International copyright secured. All rights reserved. Used by permission.

Part 2
SHARING THE GIFT

Introduction (Good News)

Graham Kendrick

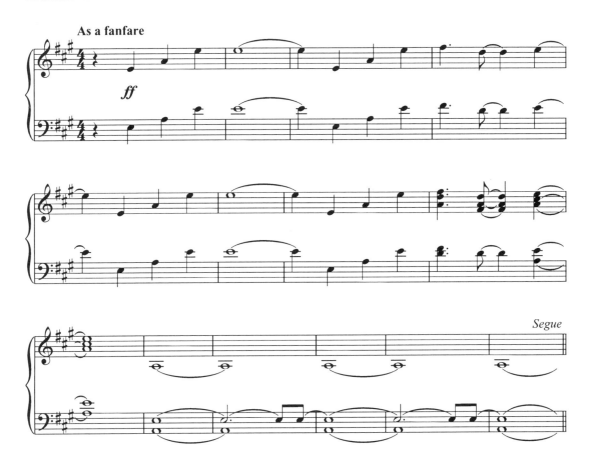

Good News

Words and Music: Graham Kendrick

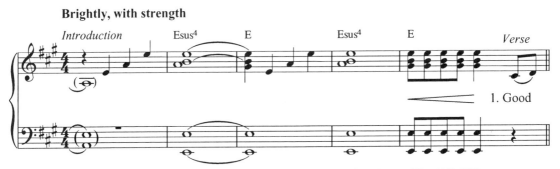

© Copyright 1988 Make Way Music, P.O. Box 263, Croydon, Surrey CR9 5AP, UK.
International copyright secured. All rights reserved. Used by permission.

Sing all the earth

Words and Music: Graham Kendrick

Gloria

Music: French or Flemish melody

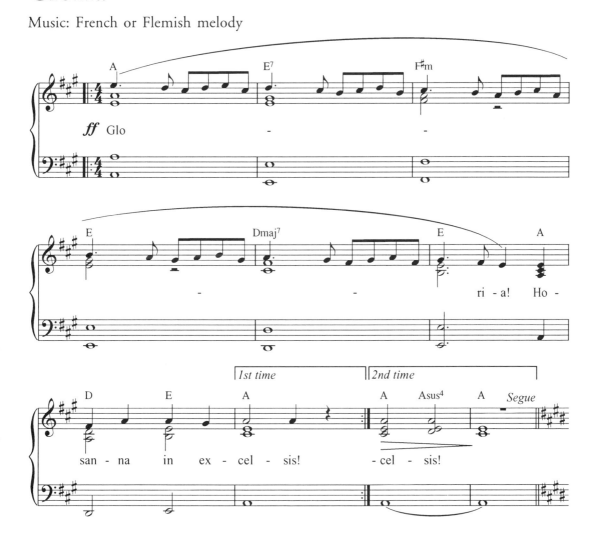

Arise, shine
Darkness like a shroud

Words and Music: Graham Kendrick

© Copyright 1985 Thankyou Music/Adm. by worshiptogether.com songs excl. UK & Europe, adm. by Kingsway Music. tym@kingsway.co.uk. Used by permission.

All: Cheers etc...

Leader says:
Welcome to the celebration!
Welcome to the greatest birthday party of all time!
We are celebrating the birth of a Child whose
coming changed the whole course of human
history, and who has changed our lives too.
Though his arrival was almost unnoticed, his birth
had been prophesied centuries before when the
prophet Isaiah said:

All say:
For a Child will be born to us, a Son will be given
to us; and he will be our ruler. He will be called
Wonderful Counsellor, Mighty God, Eternal
Father, Prince of Peace.

Leader says:
Let's celebrate together this most joyful of all
birthdays, the birthday of Jesus, the Child from
heaven.

This Child

Words and Music: Graham Kendrick

1. This Child, se-cret-ly comes in the night, oh this Child, hid-ing a hea-ven-ly light, oh this Child, com-ing to us like a stran-ger, this hea-ven-ly Child. This
2. Child, ris-ing on us like the sun, oh this Child, giv-en to light e-v'ry-one, oh this Child, guid-ing our feet on the path-way to peace on earth. This
3. Child, rais-ing the hum-ble and poor, oh this Child, mak-ing the proud ones to fall; this Child, fill-ing the hun-gry with good things, this hea-ven-ly Child. This

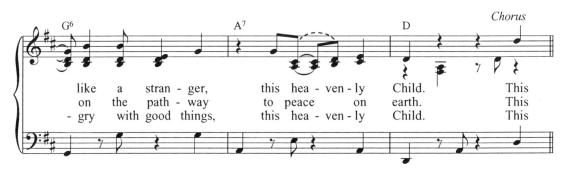

© Copyright 1988 Make Way Music, P.O. Box 263, Croydon, Surrey CR9 5AP, UK.
International copyright secured. All rights reserved. Used by permission.

Leader says:
The birth of a child should always be the cause of great rejoicing,
but how much more so when the child is none other than God himself,
come to save his people from their sins! So come and join the dance!

O come and join the dance

Words and Music: Graham Kendrick

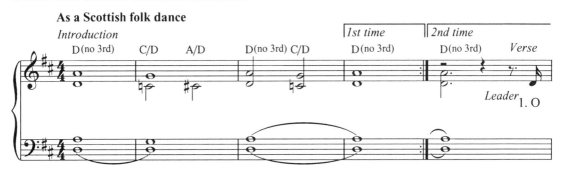

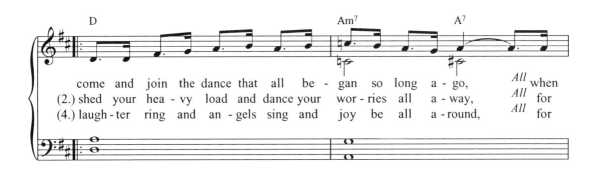

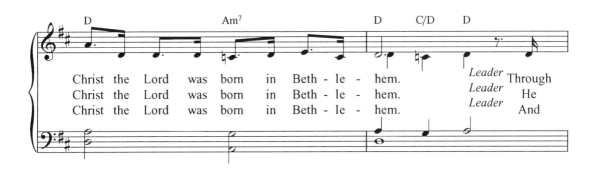

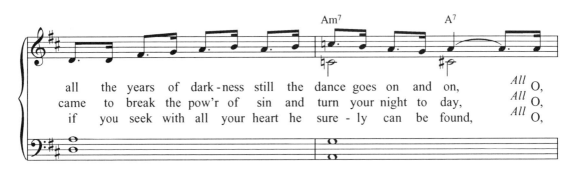

© Copyright 1988 Make Way Music, P.O. Box 263, Croydon, Surrey CR9 5AP, UK.
International copyright secured. All rights reserved. Used by permission.

Introduction (The Giving Song)

Graham Kendrick

Leader says over introduction:
On that first Christmas night, joyful angels announced peace and goodwill to the world — and heaven is still bursting at the seams with good gifts for everyone. So open your heart to receive what God has stored up for you, especially the greatest Gift of all . . .

© Copyright 1988 Make Way Music, P.O. Box 263, Croydon, Surrey CR9 5AP, UK.
International copyright secured. All rights reserved. Used by permission.

The Giving Song

Words and Music: Graham Kendrick

© Copyright 1988 Make Way Music, P.O. Box 263, Croydon, Surrey CR9 5AP, UK.
International copyright secured. All rights reserved. Used by permission.

For God so loved the world

Words and Music: Graham Kendrick

© Copyright 1988 Make Way Music, P.O. Box 263, Croydon, Surrey CR9 5AP, UK.
International copyright secured. All rights reserved. Used by permission.

Peace to you

Words and Music: Graham Kendrick

Leader says:
Let's give thanks to God together.

All say:
Thank you, heavenly Father, for the peace that comes through your gift of Jesus, the Prince of Peace. Thank you that, although he was in very nature God, he made himself as nothing, took on the nature of a servant, was made in human likeness, and experienced the pain and suffering of a sinful world.

Thank you that, in order to give us life, he humbled himself, and surrendered to death, even death on a cross...

© Copyright 1988 Make Way Music, P.O. Box 263, Croydon, Surrey CR9 5AP, UK.
International copyright secured. All rights reserved. Used by permission.

God with us

Words and Music: Graham Kendrick

© Copyright 1988 Make Way Music, P.O. Box 263, Croydon, Surrey CR9 5AP, UK.
International copyright secured. All rights reserved. Used by permission.

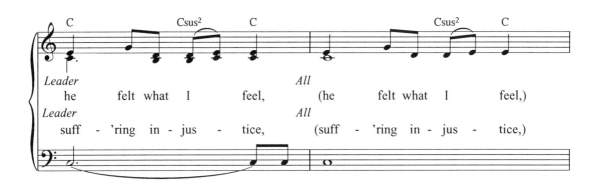
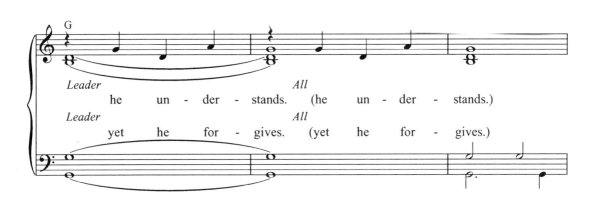
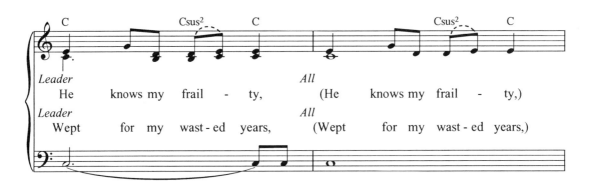
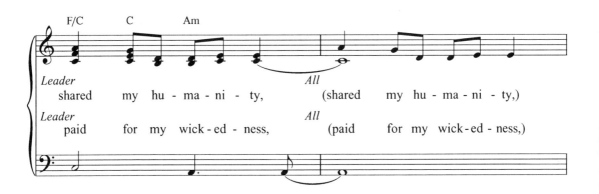

Heaven invites you to a party

Words: Graham Kendrick
 and James Montgomery (1771-1854) (*Angels, from the realms of glory*)
Music: Graham Kendrick
 and French or Flemish melody (*Angels, from the realms of glory*)

© Copyright 1988 Make Way Music, P.O. Box 263, Croydon, Surrey CR9 5AP, UK.
International copyright secured. All rights reserved. Used by permission.

Tonight (reprise)
Glory to God
Words and Music: Graham Kendrick

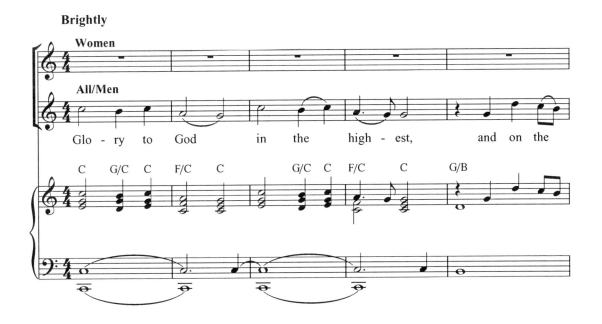

© Copyright 1988 Make Way Music, P.O. Box 263, Croydon, Surrey CR9 5AP, UK.
International copyright secured. All rights reserved. Used by permission.

Thanks be to God (reprise)

Words and Music: Graham Kendrick

WORDS

PART 1 ◆ CELEBRATING THE GIFT

TONIGHT (GLORY TO GOD)

Tonight, while all the world was sleeping,
a light exploded in the skies.
And then, as glory did surround us,
a voice, an angel did appear!

> Glory to God (MEN – WOMEN ECHO)
> in the highest, (MEN – WOMEN ECHO)
> and on the earth (MEN)
> be peace from heav'n! (ALL)
> Glory to God (MEN – WOMEN ECHO)
> in the highest, (MEN – WOMEN ECHO)
> and on the earth (MEN)
> be peace from heav'n! (ALL)

Afraid, we covered up our faces,
amazed at what our ears did hear.
Good news of joy for all the people –
today a Saviour has appeared!

> Glory to God (MEN – WOMEN ECHO)
> in the highest, (MEN – WOMEN ECHO)
> and on the earth (MEN)
> be peace from heav'n! (ALL)
> Glory to God (MEN – WOMEN ECHO)
> in the highest, (MEN – WOMEN ECHO)
> and on the earth (MEN)
> be peace from heav'n! (ALL)

And so to Bethlehem
to find it all was true;
despised and worthless shepherds,
we were the first to know!

> Glory to God (MEN – WOMEN ECHO)
> in the highest, (MEN – WOMEN ECHO)
> and on the earth (MEN)
> be peace from heav'n! (ALL)
> Glory to God (MEN – WOMEN ECHO)
> in the highest, (MEN – WOMEN ECHO)
> and on the earth (MEN)
> be peace from heav'n! (ALL)
> Glory to God (MEN – WOMEN ECHO)
> in the highest, (MEN – WOMEN ECHO)
> and on the earth (MEN)
> be peace from heav'n! (ALL)
> Glory to God (MEN – WOMEN ECHO)
> in the highest, (MEN – WOMEN ECHO)
> and on the earth (MEN)
> be peace from heav'n! (ALL)

Graham Kendrick
Copyright © 1988 Make Way Music

THE CHRISTMAS CHILD

Hear the sound of people singing,
all the bells are ringing
for the Christmas Child.
In the streets the lights are glowing,
but there is no knowing
of the Christmas Child.

> *Oh, let this Child be born in your heart,*
> *oh, let this Child be born in your heart,*
> *tonight, tonight,*
> *tonight, tonight.*

Will our wars go on for ever,
and will peace be never
at Christmastime?
If we keep him in the manger
then there is no danger
from the Christmas Child.

> *Oh, let this Child be born in your heart,*
> *oh, let this Child be born in your heart,*
> *tonight, tonight,*
> *tonight, tonight.*

*Oh, let this Child be born in your heart,
oh, let this Child be born in your heart,
tonight, tonight,
tonight, tonight.*

THE SERVANT KING

From heaven you came, helpless babe,
entered our world, your glory veiled;
not to be served but to serve,
and give your life that we might live.

> *This is our God, the Servant King.
> He calls us now to follow him,
> to bring our lives as a daily offering
> of worship to the Servant King.*

LET IT BE TO ME

Let it be to me
according to your word.
Let it be to me
according to your word.

I am your servant,
no rights shall I demand.
Let it be to me,
let it be to me,
let it be to me
according to your word.

I am your servant,
no rights shall I demand.
Let it be to me,
let it be to me,
let it be to me
according to your word.

IMMANUEL, O IMMANUEL

Immanuel, O Immanuel,
bowed in awe I worship at your feet,
and sing Immanuel, God is with us,
sharing my humanness, my shame,
feeling my weaknesses, my pain,
taking the punishment, the blame,
Immanuel.
And now my words cannot explain,
all that my heart cannot contain,
how great are the glories of your name,
Immanuel.

Immanuel, O Immanuel,
bowed in awe I worship at your feet,
and sing Immanuel, God is with us,
sharing my humanness, my shame,
feeling my weaknesses, my pain,
taking the punishment, the blame,
Immanuel.
And now my words cannot explain,
all that my heart cannot contain,
how great are the glories of your name,
Immanuel,
Immanuel,
Immanuel,
Immanuel.

THANKS BE TO GOD

Father, never was love so near;
tender, my deepest wounds to heal.
Precious to me, your gift of love;
for me you gave your only Son.

> *And now thanks be to God
> for his gift beyond words,
> the Son whom he loved,
> no, he did not withhold him,
> but with him gave everything.
> Now he's everything to me.*

(continued overleaf)

Jesus, the heart of God revealed,
with us, feeling the pain we feel.
Cut to the heart, wounded for me,
taking the blame, making me clean.

And now thanks be to God
for his gift beyond words,
the Son whom he loved,
no, he did not withhold him,
but with him gave everything.
Now he's everything to me.

And now thanks be to God
for his gift beyond words,
the Son whom he loved,
no, he did not withhold him,
but with him gave everything.
Now he's everything to me.

Graham Kendrick
Copyright © 1988 Make Way Music

O WHAT A MYSTERY I SEE

O what a mystery I see,
what marvellous design,
that God should come as one of us,
a Son in David's line.
Flesh of our flesh, of woman born,
our humanness he owns;
and for a world of wickedness
his guiltless blood atones.

This perfect Man, incarnate God,
by selfless sacrifice
destroyed our sinful history,
all fallen Adam's curse.
In him the curse to blessing turns,
my barren spirit flowers,
as over the shattered power of sin
the cross of Jesus towers.

(WOMEN)
By faith a child of his I stand,
an heir in David's line,
royal descendant by his blood
destined by Love's design.
(MEN)
Fathers of faith, my fathers now!
Because in Christ I am,
(ALL)
and all God's promises in him
to me are 'Yes, Amen'!

No more then as a child of earth
must I my lifetime spend –
his history, his destiny
are mine to apprehend.
Oh what a Saviour, what a Lord,
O Master, Brother, Friend!
What miracle has joined me to
this life that never ends!

Graham Kendrick
Copyright © 1988 Make Way Music

TELL OUT, TELL OUT THE NEWS

Now dawns the sun of righteousness,
and the darkness shall never
his brightness dim;
true light that lights the hearts of men,
only Son of the Father, Jesus Christ.

Tell out, tell out the news,
on every street proclaim
a child is born, a Son is given,
and Jesus is his name!
Tell out, tell out the news,
our Saviour Christ has come,
in every tribe and nation
let songs of praise be sung,
let songs of praise be sung!

Laughter and joy he will increase,
all our burdens be lifted,
oppression cease;
the blood-stained battle-dress be burned,
and the art of our warfare
nevermore be learned.

*Tell out, tell out the news,
on every street proclaim
a child is born, a Son is given,
and Jesus is his name!
Tell out, tell out the news,
our Saviour Christ has come,
in every tribe and nation
let songs of praise be sung,
let songs of praise be sung!*

So let us go, his witnesses,
spreading news of his kingdom
of righteousness,
'til the whole world has heard the song,
'til the harvest is gathered,
then the end shall come.

*Tell out, tell out the news,
on every street proclaim
a child is born, a Son is given,
and Jesus is his name!
Tell out, tell out the news,
our Saviour Christ has come,
in every tribe and nation
let songs of praise be sung,
let songs of praise be sung!*

Graham Kendrick
Copyright © 1988 Make Way Music

THE CANDLE SONG

Like a candle flame,
flick'ring small
in our darkness.
Uncreated light
shines through infant eyes.

God is with us,	(MEN – WOMEN ECHO)
alleluia,	(MEN – WOMEN ECHO)
come to save us,	(MEN – WOMEN ECHO)
alleluia,	(MEN – WOMEN ECHO)
alleluia!	(ALL)

Stars and angels sing,
yet the earth
sleeps in shadows;
can this tiny spark
set a world on fire?

God is with us,	(MEN – WOMEN ECHO)
alleluia,	(MEN – WOMEN ECHO)
come to save us,	(MEN – WOMEN ECHO)
alleluia,	(MEN – WOMEN ECHO)
alleluia!	(ALL)

Yet his light will shine
from our lives,
Spirit blazing,
as we touch the flame
of his holy fire.

God is with us,	(MEN – WOMEN ECHO)
alleluia,	(MEN – WOMEN ECHO)
come to save us,	(MEN – WOMEN ECHO)
alleluia,	(MEN – WOMEN ECHO)
alleluia!	(ALL)

God is with us,	(MEN – WOMEN ECHO)
alleluia,	(MEN – WOMEN ECHO)
come to save us,	(MEN – WOMEN ECHO)
alleluia,	(MEN – WOMEN ECHO)
alleluia!	(ALL)

Graham Kendrick
Copyright © 1988 Make Way Music

PART 2 ◆ SHARING THE GIFT

GOOD NEWS

Good news, good news to you we bring,
alleluia!
News of great joy that angels sing,
alleluia!

> *Tender mercy he has shown us,*
> *joy to all the world;*
> *for us God sends his only Son,*
> *alleluia!*

Let earth's dark shadows fly away,
alleluia!
In Christ has dawned an endless day,
alleluia!

> *Tender mercy he has shown us,*
> *joy to all the world;*
> *for us God sends his only Son,*
> *alleluia!*

Now God with us on earth resides,
alleluia!
And heaven's door is open wide,
alleluia!

> *Tender mercy he has shown us,*
> *joy to all the world;*
> *for us God sends his only Son,*
> *alleluia!*

Graham Kendrick
Copyright © 1988 Make Way Music

SING ALL THE EARTH/GLORIA

Sing, all the earth,
for the Lord,
he has come among us,
sing all the earth,
sing all the earth.

(MEN – WOMEN ECHO)
Sing, all the earth
for the Lord,
he has come among us,
sing all the earth,
sing all the earth.

Come, all you citizens,
welcome your God and
  Creator,   (MEN – WOMEN ECHO)
sing all the earth,   (ALL)
sing all the earth.   (ALL)

Gloria!
Hosanna in excelsis!
Gloria
Hosanna in excelsis!

Graham Kendrick
Copyright © 1988 Make Way Music
'Gloria' words by G R Woodward (1848-1934)

ARISE, SHINE

Darkness like a shroud covers the earth;
evil like a cloud covers the people.
But the Lord will rise upon you,
and his glory will appear on you –
nations will come to your light.

> *Arise, shine, your light has come,*
> *the glory of the Lord has risen on you!*
> *Arise, shine, your light has come,*
> *Jesus the Light of the world has come.*

Here among us now, Christ the Light
kindles brighter flames in our trembling
  hearts!
Living Word, our Lamp, come guide our
  feet
as we walk as one in light and peace,
'til justice and truth shine like the sun.

*Arise, shine, your light has come,
the glory of the Lord has risen on you!
Arise, shine, your light has come,
Jesus the Light of the world has come!*

Your light has come!	(MEN)
Your light has come!	(WOMEN)
Your light has come!	(MEN)
Your light has come!	(WOMEN)
Your light has come!	(ALL)

Graham Kendrick
Copyright © 1985 Thankyou Music

ALL: Cheers, etc . . .

LEADER SAYS:
Welcome to the celebration!
Welcome to the greatest birthday party of all time!
We are celebrating the birth of a Child whose coming changed the whole course of human history, and who has changed our lives too.
Though his arrival was almost unnoticed, his birth had been prophesied centuries before when the prophet Isaiah said:

ALL SAY:
For a Child will be born to us, a Son will be given to us; and he will be our ruler.
He will be called Wonderful Counsellor, Mighty God, Eternal Father, Prince of Peace.

LEADER SAYS:
Let's celebrate together this most joyful of all birthdays, the birthday of Jesus, the Child from heaven.

THIS CHILD

This Child, secretly comes in the night,
oh this Child, hiding a heavenly light,
oh this Child, coming to us like a stranger,
this heavenly Child.

*This Child, heaven come down now
to be with us here,
heavenly love and mercy appear,
softly in awe and wonder come near
to this heavenly Child.*

This Child, rising on us like the sun,
oh this Child, given to light everyone,
oh this Child, guiding our feet on the pathway
to peace on earth.

*This Child, heaven come down now
to be with us here,
heavenly love and mercy appear,
softly in awe and wonder come near
to this heavenly Child.*

This Child, raising the humble and poor,
oh this Child, making the proud ones to fall;
this Child, filling the hungry with good things,
this heavenly Child.

*This Child, heaven come down now
to be with us here,
heavenly love and mercy appear,
softly in awe and wonder come near
to this heavenly Child.*

*This Child, heaven come down now
to be with us here,
heavenly love and mercy appear,
softly in awe and wonder come near
to this heavenly Child.*

Graham Kendrick
Copyright © 1988 Make Way Music

LEADER SAYS:
The birth of a child should always be the cause of great rejoicing, but how much more so when the child is none other than God himself, come to save his people from their sins!
So come and join the dance!

O COME AND JOIN THE DANCE

LDR: O come and join the dance
that all began so long ago,
ALL: when Christ the Lord was born in Bethlehem.
LDR: Through all the years of darkness
still the dance goes on and on,
ALL: O, take my hand and come and join the song.

MEN: *Rejoice!* (WOMEN ECHO)
Rejoice! (WOMEN ECHO)
ALL: *O lift your voice and sing,
and open up your heart to welcome him.*
MEN: *Rejoice!* (WOMEN ECHO)
Rejoice! (WOMEN ECHO)
ALL: *and welcome now your King,
for Christ the Lord was born in Bethlehem.*

LDR: Come shed your heavy load
and dance your worries all away,
ALL: for Christ the Lord was born in Bethlehem.
LDR: He came to break the power of sin
and turn your night to day,
ALL: O, take my hand and come and join the song.

MEN: *Rejoice!* (WOMEN ECHO)
Rejoice! (WOMEN ECHO)
ALL: *O lift your voice and sing,
and open up your heart to welcome him.*
MEN: *Rejoice!* (WOMEN ECHO)
Rejoice! (WOMEN ECHO)
ALL: *and welcome now your King,
for Christ the Lord was born in Bethlehem.*

(INSTRUMENTAL VERSE AND CHORUS)

LDR: Let laughter ring and angels sing
and joy be all around,
ALL: for Christ the Lord was born in Bethlehem.
LDR: And if you seek with all your heart
he surely can be found,
ALL: O, take my hand and come and join the song.

MEN: *Rejoice!* (WOMEN ECHO)
Rejoice! (WOMEN ECHO)
ALL: *O lift your voice and sing,
and open up your heart to welcome him.*
MEN: *Rejoice!* (WOMEN ECHO)
Rejoice! (WOMEN ECHO)
ALL: *and welcome now your King,
for Christ the Lord was born in Bethlehem.*

MEN: *Rejoice!* (WOMEN ECHO)
Rejoice! (WOMEN ECHO)
ALL: *O lift your voice and sing,
and open up your heart to welcome him.*
MEN: *Rejoice!* (WOMEN ECHO)
Rejoice! (WOMEN ECHO)
ALL: *and welcome now your King,
for Christ the Lord was born in Bethlehem.
For Christ the Lord was born in Bethlehem.
For Christ the Lord was born in Bethlehem.*

Graham Kendrick
Copyright © 1988 Make Way Music

LEADER SAYS OVER INTRODUCTION:
On that first Christmas night, joyful angels announced peace and goodwill to the world – and heaven is still bursting at the seams with good gifts for everyone.
So open your heart to receive what God has stored up for you, especially the greatest Gift of all . . .

THE GIVING SONG

*At this time of giving,
gladly now we bring
gifts of goodness and mercy
from a heavenly King.*

Earth could not contain the treasures
heaven holds for you;
perfect joy and lasting pleasures,
love so strong and true.

*At this time of giving,
gladly now we bring
gifts of goodness and mercy
from a heavenly King.*

May his tender love surround you
at this Christmastime;
may you see his smiling face
that in the darkness shines.

*At this time of giving,
gladly now we bring
gifts of goodness and mercy
from a heavenly King.*

But the many gifts he gives
are all poured out from one;
come receive the greatest gift,
the gift of God's own Son.

Lai, lai, lai . . .   (FOR TWO CHORUSES AND VERSES)

Graham Kendrick
Copyright © 1988 Make Way Music

FOR GOD SO LOVED THE WORLD

For God so loved the world
that he gave his only Son;
and all who believe on him
shall not die,
but have eternal life;
no, they shall not die,
but have eternal life.

And God showed his love for you,
when he gave his only Son;
and you, if you trust in him,
shall not die,
but have eternal life;
no, you shall not die,
but have eternal life.

Graham Kendrick
Copyright © 1988 Make Way Music

PEACE TO YOU

Peace to you.
We bless you now in the name of the
   Lord.
Peace to you.
We bless you now in the name of the
   Prince of Peace.
Peace to you.
(REPEAT TWICE)

Peace to you.
We bless you now in the name of the
   Lord.
Peace to you.
We bless you now in the name of the
   Prince of Peace.
Peace to you, peace to you.
Peace to you, peace to you.

Graham Kendrick
Copyright © 1988 Make Way Music

LEADER SAYS:
Let's give thanks to God together.

ALL SAY:
Thank you, heavenly Father, for the
   peace that comes through your gift of
   Jesus, the Prince of Peace.
Thank you that, although he was in very
   nature God, he made himself as
   nothing, took on the nature of a
   servant, was made in human likeness,
   and experienced the pain and suffering
   of a sinful world.

(continued overleaf)

Thank you that, in order to give us life,
he humbled himself, and surrendered
to death, even death on a cross . . .

GOD WITH US

LDR: He walked where I walk,
(ALL ECHO EACH LINE)
he stood where I stand,
he felt what I feel,
he understands.
He knows my frailty,
shared my humanity,
tempted in every way,
yet without sin.

ALL: God with us, so close to us,
God with us, Immanuel!
God with us, so close to us,
God with us, Immanuel!

LDR: One of a hated race,
(ALL ECHO EACH LINE)
stung by the prejudice,
suff'ring injustice,
yet he forgives.
Wept for my wasted years,
paid for my wickedness,
he died in my place,
that I might live.

All: God with us, so close to us,
God with us, Immanuel!
God with us, so close to us,
God with us, Immanuel!

All: God with us, so close to us,
God with us, Immanuel!
God with us, so close to us,
God with us, Immanuel!

Graham Kendrick
Copyright © 1988 Make Way Music

HEAVEN INVITES YOU TO A PARTY

Heaven invites you to a party,
to celebrate the birth of a Son;
angels rejoicing in the starlight,
singing 'Christ your Saviour has come'.

Heaven invites you to a party,
to celebrate the birth of a Son;
angels rejoicing in the starlight,
singing 'Christ your Saviour has come'.

(LEADER FIRST, ALL ECHO EACH LINE)
And it's for you,
and it's for me,
for all your friends
and family.
Now heaven's door
is open wide,
so come on in,
come step inside.

Heaven invites you to a party,
to celebrate the birth of a Son;
angels rejoicing in the starlight,
singing 'Christ your Saviour has come'.

ALL: Angels, from the realms of glory,
wing your flight o'er all the earth;
you who sang creation's story,
now proclaim Messiah's birth.

(LEADER FIRST, ALL ECHO EACH LINE)
And it's for you,
and it's for me,
for all your friends
and family.
Let trumpets blast,
let music play,
let people shout,
let banners wave.

(LEADER FIRST, ALL ECHO EACH LINE)
Come all you people,
join hands together,
bring all your neighbours,
everybody!
Send invitations,
to every nation,
come and adore him,
everybody!
Everybody!

ALL:
Heaven invites you to a party,
to celebrate the birth of a Son;
angels rejoicing in the starlight,
singing 'Christ your Saviour has come'.

(LEADER FIRST, ALL ECHO EACH LINE)
And it's for you,
and it's for me,
for all your friends
and family.
Let trumpets blast,
let music play,
let people shout,
let banners wave.

Graham Kendrick
Copyright © 1988 Make Way Music
'Angels from the realms of glory' words by J. Montgomery (1771-1854)

TONIGHT (GLORY TO GOD) (Reprise)

*Glory to God
in the highest,
and on the earth
be peace from heav'n!*

*Glory to God
in the highest,
and on the earth
be peace from heav'n!*

Glory to God (MEN – WOMEN ECHO)
in the highest, (MEN – WOMEN ECHO)
and on the earth (MEN)
be peace from heav'n! (ALL)

Glory to God (MEN – WOMEN ECHO)
in the highest, (MEN – WOMEN ECHO)
and on the earth (MEN)
be peace from heav'n! (ALL)

Graham Kendrick
Copyright © 1988 Make Way Music

THANKS BE TO GOD (Reprise)

*And now thanks be to God
for his gift beyond words,
the Son whom he loved,
no, he did not withhold him,
but with him gave everything.
Now he's everything to me.
Now he's everything to me.*

Glory to God in the highest!

Graham Kendrick
Copyright © 1988 Make Way Music

Also available from
KEVIN MAYHEW PUBLISHING...

Rumours of Angels
Graham Kendrick

Guitar/keyboard	1450193	ISBN 1 84003 616 8
Choir/organ	1450192	ISBN 1 84003 617 6

This is a wonderful worship musical for the Christmas season. It is ideal for performance at any time from the beginning of Advent until Epiphany and will provide a thrilling experience for both performers and congregation.

Graham Kendrick, one of the greatest names in contemporary church music, provides a challenging scripture-based text and melodies of great beauty and strength. *Rumours of Angels* has been performed successfully on numerous occasions and we are pleased to publish these entirely reset editions.

Rumours of Angels is a continuous work with 11 pieces. It is easily within the competence of the average worship group or parish choir.

We have published two versions of *Rumours of Angels*:
- *Guitar/keyboard* is suitable for worship groups
- *Choir/organ* is a fine choral version arranged by David Terry

The 11 songs of *Rumours of Angels* are:
Can you believe it
Rumours of Angels
Earth lies spellbound
Nothing will ever be the same again
Thorns in the straw
Ain't nothing like it
Seekers and dreamers
He is here
What kind of greatness
You came from the highest
White horse